To Matt, Ruby & Daisy
– Kathy Weller

"The Months" was first published in *Pretty Lessons in Verse for Good Children* (1834) by Sara Coleridge.
This Illustrated Edition © 2007 Lobster Press
Illustrations © 2007 Kathy Weller

Published by Lobster Press™
1620 Sherbrooke Street West, Suites C & D
Montréal, Québec   H3H 1C9
Tel. (514) 904-1100 • Fax (514) 904-1101
www.lobsterpress.com

Publisher: Alison Fripp
Editors: Alison Fripp & Meghan Nolan
Editorial Assistant: Faye Smailes
Graphic Design & Production: Tammy Desnoyers

Société
de développement
des entreprises
culturelles
Québec ⊞⊞

We acknowledge the support of the government of Québec,
tax credit for book publishing, administered by SODEC.

Library and Archives Canada Cataloguing in Publication

Coleridge, Sara, 1802-1852.
    The months : fun with friends all year 'round / Sara Coleridge ; illustrations by Kathy Weller.

(Read me a poem)
ISBN 978-1-897073-67-4

    I. Weller, Kathy, 1969- II. Title. III. Series.

PR4489.C2M66 2007   j821'.7   C2007-901572-7

Printed and bound in Malaysia.

The **Months**

a poem by **Sara Coleridge**

Fun with Friends
All Year 'Round!

illustrated by **Kathy Weller**

Lobster Press ™

January brings

the snow,

Makes our feet

and fingers glow.

February brings

the rain,

Thaws the frozen

lake again.

March brings

breezes loud

and shrill,

Stirs the dancing

daffodil.

April brings

the primrose sweet,

Scatters daisies

at our feet.

May brings

flocks of pretty lambs,

Skipping by their

fleecy dams.

June brings

tulips, lilies, roses,

Fills the children's

hands with posies.

Hot

July brings

cooling showers,

Apricots and

gillyflowers.

August brings

the sheaves of corn,

Then the harvest

home is borne.

Warm

September brings

the fruit,

Sportsmen then

begin to shoot.

Fresh

October brings

the pheasant,

Then to gather nuts

is pleasant.

Dull

November brings

the blast,

Then the leaves

are whirling fast.

Chill **December** brings
the sleet,
Blazing fire, and
Christmas treat.